The Right Mind For Golf

Overcoming golf's mental challenges
and the mastering of your mental game

Barry Lotz, J.D., Ph.D.

First published in 2011, Sixth Printing 2017

ISBN: 978-0-9705228-7-0

ALSO BY DR. BARRY LOTZ:

Enforcing Difficult Judgments

America's Last Great Real Estate Secret - Tax Sales

Earn $250 an Hour, No Experience Required, Government Approved

Business Arbitration and Debt Negotiation

Investing in Judgment Liens

Competency is the Ability of Dance During Breakdown™— 201 Ways to Improve your Company's Bottom Line

Factoring—The Financing Tool of the 90's

Skip Tracing Made Easy

333 Best Web Sites for Golfers

333 Best Web Sites for The Female Business Executive

333 Best Web Sites for The Business Executive

Investing In Distressed Credit Card Paper

101 Other Uses for Your Law Degree

How To Build Business Relationships Through Golf

A SPECIAL THANKS TO:

Susie Lotz for her motivation, unqualified and boundless love, plus her excellent proof reading skills

Aaron and Jonathan Lotz for their positive attitudes in life and their unwavering love and support

Rich Katz for his encouragement and friendship

Dr. Patrick Cohn for his training, professionalism and mentoring

Mike Kletz for his K.I.S.S. Keep It Superbly Simple theories

To the Tour players and their caddies

And to all the golfers throughout the world who want to improve their mental game:

Relax

Focus

Commit

Execute

Enjoy the journey

Always ask yourself, "What did I learn? What am I doing right?"

Optimism + Gratitude - Ego = Success

CONTENTS

FOREWORD

The only person who can allow you to achieve the future you desire and deserve is YOU!

You are worthy. You deserve to be happy. You can achieve your goals. You are special. You can do anything you want to do. You deserve to be who you want to be.

Surround yourself with positive people and fill your mind with positive information, which will encourage you to be enthusiastic and pursue your dreams. These people may not be able to provide advice that directly helps you reach your goals, but they can provide encouragement when you feel frustrated and offer advice when you feel you can't go on anymore.

Motivated people push you closer toward your goals through their encouragement and advice, while negative people will always tell you why something will not work.

I'm not saying you need to start listening to motivational audios or take on any extra commitments. It might be as simple as dropping some current negative time-wasting activities. Maybe spend less time with the most negative people in your life, or ask them to change the topic of their conversations. Also, remember that "competency is the ability to dance during breakdown" (c).

Successful individuals know the secrets of mental game success in their chosen sport. They reached the pinnacle of their sport, not only because they had the physical ability, the desire and the opportunities, but because of a powerful mental game! The mental game is just as important as the physical, if not more and has helped every successful athlete rise to the top.

DR. BARRY LOTZ

INTRODUCTION

I've got a simple fact for you to consider—even though 90% of the game of golf is mental, we only spend about 10% of our time training our minds to play golf. This is true for golfers of every level, from amateurs to pros.

And consider this—how long does it take for you to make a golf swing? About 2 seconds tops. So, what are you doing the rest of the 4 or 5 hours you're on the course? I think we've gotten a little confused in our training approach!

The purpose of this book is to create the "right mind" for golf—one that is impenetrable, incapable of being damaged or harmed, and impossible to distract. The right mind for golf is calm, relaxed and impervious to distraction. It is focused solely on making the perfect shot, getting the ball to its target, and victory on the golf course.

The right mind for golf is a joyous one!

In this book, I'm giving you 10 Golden Rules that will help you discover what you want and need to learn. You can also use meditation techniques and self-hypnosis to get even better results. I'll explain a bit more about them later.

When you start achieving success and gaining the desired results, you'll be that much more motivated to commit to these rules—to practice them, master them and ingrain them into your golfing life. The only person who can allow you to achieve the future you desire and deserve is YOU! And you can even apply these rules to other things in your life outside of your golf game— what a deal!

THE GOLDEN RULES THAT
WILL MAKE IT HAPPEN:

1. Now Is How—How to live in the moment

2. You Are In Control—Learn how to manage your own thoughts

3. Relax, Commit and Execute—How to try less and perform better

4. Trust Yourself—Trust your mind, keep it simple and stay positive

5. Focus—How to focus on success instead of failure

6. Your Inner Confidence—How to access your inner confidence whenever you need it

7. Meaning—Nothing has any meaning except the meaning you give it

8. Breathing—How to breathe with your eyes

9. Your Success Scorecard—Keeping track of your successes

10. The Problem With Perfection—What's wrong with perfection and why you should never give up

As you become more familiar with these Golden Rules, you'll see how meditation and hypnosis let you access the kind of mindset you need when you take to the course.

With golf, everything depends on your state of mind. Most of us think that you play golf to relax, but this is dead wrong—You have to relax to play golf!

So, if you can train your mind to let go of thoughts that don't serve you, and instead make use of the ones that do, you become more relaxed and better able to maintain focus. This focus helps you to perform the tasks you need in order to play golf well. A relaxed golfer is a better golfer because they don't let anxieties and worries interrupt the flow of the game.

Of course, you can't always get rid of negative thoughts before you pick up your clubs. You also can't always swing all the way from negative to positive. However, you absolutely can learn how to return to a neutral, naturally focused state quickly and easily. Sometimes self-hypnosis helps to achieve this. By using hypnosis to do this, you allow yourself enough time to get your mind where it needs to be.

An equally effective alternative to hypnosis is TM, or transcendental meditation. If you practice TM twice a day for 20 minutes, you'll experience phenomenal clarity, reduced stress and overall well-being for both mind and body. Having personally been a devotee of TM for the past 30 years, I can honestly tell you that it's a wonderful tool in one's arsenal to keep you positive and balanced.

Whether you use hypnosis by a licensed professional, self-hypnosis or TM, your mind will be trained to provide the level of relaxation that you need. These methods unlock the subconscious mind. They help you to build a mind that is consistently resistant to stress and anxiety.

SOME BACKGROUND ON HYPNOSIS

You can't work with something you don't understand, so here is a little background on hypnosis to help you get more out of it. The physiological and psychological benefits of hypnosis are widely known. Hypnosis puts you into a natural state of mind that helps to quell fears and give you a natural means of achieving both physical and mental control.

Your subconscious mind has a huge influence on everything you do every day, but you've got little control over it. It's actually more influential than your everyday conscious mind. This is your regular wakeful state. If you can access your subconscious mind, you can get into that deep relaxed state that you need to perform at your best. Hypnosis offer this pathway.

Your critical, analytical conscious mind often blocks the subconscious mind, and that's the one we really need. But through hypnosis, you can access it anywhere anytime. It is actually much more powerful than your conscious mind, but it doesn't always speak so loudly.

For example, think about walking. There is no way that you could consciously deal with making all the countless muscle movements or maintaining your balance when you walk. Your subconscious handles it for you quietly and effectively.

Tasks that are more complex than walking require even more tiny subconscious movements. Consider for a moment reaching for a glass of water, driving a car or swinging your golf club! Can you see how powerful the subconscious is? It can handle 40 million bits of data per minute, while your conscious mind can barely handle 40!

Once we learn a basic task as children, it is committed to our subconscious where it runs like a tape, playing the same thing over and over again, until it is either changed or re-recorded.

Now, let's apply this to the golf course—How many times have you repeated exactly the same behavior that you know consciously is the wrong, non-functional thing to do? That's the power of your subconscious.

The reason we don't stop is because the program is sealed in the subconscious and it dutifully plays on. As powerful as it is, the subconscious is undiscerning. It doesn't judge things to be good or bad, real or unreal. It simply plays the same tune in response to some external stimulus, no questions asked.

When we react out of past experiences, we are responding to behavior triggers. These behavior triggers also affect your golf game. It's as if all the things that happened in the past are permanently recorded in the pathways of your subconscious mind. Chances are, you'll feel and react instantly in the same way to your behavior triggers, and you won't even be aware of it.

Hypnosis is so successful at changing unwanted behaviors and creating new ones because it accesses the subconscious mind and allows the old tapes to be re-recorded.

We sometimes call hypnosis "meditation with a purpose." It can also be referred to as highly-focused concentration. In hypnosis, you bypass your critical conscious mind and communicate directly with the subconscious. If you practice hypnosis on a regular basis, it will give you peace so deep and tranquil that it might be hard to return to the familiar world!

What it can do for you depends largely on what you want it to do. The process for using hypnosis to improve your life—both on and off the golf course—will likely include the following key touchstones:

○ Have a goal

○ Have an obsessive desire to achieve that goal

○ Have a plan for achieving that goal through continuous, consistent effort

○ Be able to tightly close your mind against all negative and discouraging thoughts and influences

○ Have an unquestionable belief that you will succeed

SEE STEPS TO PERFORM SELF HYPNOSIS ON PAGE 91

SOME BACKGROUND ON TM— TRANSCENDENTAL MEDITATION

Transcendental Meditation is a simple, effective technique that enlivens the unlimited potential of life from its source in the unified field. To put it in a way that's easier to understand, it enriches every single area of your life, just like watering the root of a plant brings nourishment to all its parts.

Over 4 million people all over the world practice Transcendental Meditation, including more than 1 million people in the United States. People who practice TM include every age, profession, educational background and religious practice. And the number keeps growing.

Over 6,000 doctors in the United States have learned the technique of Transcendental Meditation. It's also used by tens of thousands of executives, managers and employees of companies from the smallest businesses to the largest corporations all over the world. TM is practiced by athletes, attorneys, computer programmers, teachers, students, sales clerks, clergy, factory workers, homemakers, architects, airline pilots, electricians, chefs, artists—in other words, all walks of life.

Why? Because Transcendental Meditation is easy to learn and it works. Anybody can get great benefits from it.

Studies have recently been carried out in over 210 universities and research institutions in 33 countries worldwide on the effects of TM. Many of these over 500 studies have been published in scientific journals. The results they've found from practicing TM include:

- O Reduces stress levels

- O Increases creativity and intelligence

- ○ Improves memory and learning ability

- ○ Increases physical and mental energy

- ○ Increases inner calm

- ○ Reduces insomnia

- ○ Increases feelings of happiness and self-esteem

- ○ Reduces anxiety and depression

- ○ Improves relationships with friends and loved ones

- ○ Improves overall health

- ○ Promotes a younger biological age

THE RIGHT MIND FOR GOLF

"You just have to stay in the moment. Golf is one shot at a time. You cannot live in the past. You have to play the shot at hand. That's what I've always done."

-Tiger Woods

"My main goal starting the day was to go out there and win the golf tournament."

-Vijay Singh

Now Is How—The Ram Dass Theory of Living in the Moment

As each moment unfolds, it is a moment of power. If you live in the moment, you can tap into this power. This power is infinite and it opens up potential that would otherwise be lost. Forget the notion that the past equals the future; if you think that way, you miss the power of right now, and its full potential to give you the most out of every moment of your life.

Don't let the past weigh you down on what you are doing in the present. In golfing parlay, this translates to isolating each hole, regardless of how you felt when you walked off the previous green.

Doubts cloud the mind's power. If you want to bring your mind to the present, you have to erase this doubt. A mind without doubt is a more powerful mind. More importantly, you need to learn to quiet your mind and trust your instincts and intuition. You have to slow it all down. This will make you more energetic, alert, and also relaxed.

Think about where you are right now, as you read this. You're probably sitting comfortably somewhere with food in your belly and a shelter over your head. All is well. Your only obstacles to this feeling of well-being are the stressful thoughts that can push their way in.

If you have guilt, fear or sadness, these feelings can color your thinking and steal your focus away. We've all been conditioned to accept these things—largely as a result of everyday life stresses like work, family, illness and the roles we must play—as the normal state of living. We're so good at functioning with these stresses that we've come to accept them as our constant companions.

But this is not normal at all! There is no reason why life should be experienced this way. Stress always deals with what is ahead of us or behind us, not with what we face now. So, forget about them. Change your view and look at the present.

GROUNDING AND BALANCE

In order to relieve yourself of doubt and live a more natural life where you can make better, clearer decisions, you need balance. If you are in harmony, life is much smoother. Getting into a state of balance makes dramatic improvements. To improve your golf game and all of your everyday functioning, you must get into the right balance.

There are two ways we achieve balance—grounding the body and finding the center. Being grounded simply means to be in the here and now. It means having your energy field present in your body at the present time, connected clearly to your present identity and aware of what is happening around you.

Grounding keeps your body safe from outside forces that attack it and cause it stress. Your body is a sacred temple, and grounding keeps it safe. It also increases your spiritual and energetic awareness.

Grounding is very simple—it requires placing both feet firmly on the ground. You will feel how your body physically connects you to the Earth. Standing this way, imagine roots going from your feet down into the Earth. This gives you the feeling of having a solid foundation. This is an easy daily exercise that can be done anywhere and anytime—even if you're filling your car with gas!

Next, let's look at finding your center. As you're grounding yourself, notice where your energy is centered. Is it in your chest, legs or head? Take this energy and focus it to the spot two inches below your navel, in between the front and back of your body.

This is the solar plexus, and in martial arts it's considered the center of the body. In Chinese it is called *dantien*, and in Japanese *hara*. Breathe deeply and focus on inhaling and exhaling from this center. Feel your life-force energy (chi) as it flows from this center to the rest of your body, connecting all of its parts.

Now is how—not just in golf, but in everything. Instead of mentally traveling back to the past or projecting yourself into the future, be here now in the moment. Flipping between future and past tends to fragment your thinking. Instead, focus only on this moment, and on how complete and perfect it is. Take the time to harness the power of this moment.

As you play, only you know the degree to which these everyday stresses affect your game. I encourage you to allow stressful events to affect you only as they occur. Don't drag them around with you. Don't relive them in your mind. Deal with them in real time, then move on. Once you begin to regularly do this, your stressful thoughts will let go of you while you let go of them.

Bring this thinking with you onto the course. As you walk the fairway or line up for a shot, collect your entire self into that moment. Free yourself from thoughts of the past or future, and remain firmly in the present. Instead of thinking of your last game or shot, or anticipating what will happen with the next one, stay right here in this perfect moment.

In doing so, you will harness the power of your mind—your newly clear, unencumbered mind— and will communicate that power to your body. You'll be surer of what you're doing. Being in the now takes your skill and enhances it. You can devote more attention to it than ever before, to refine it that much more. This most certainly will improve your game.

"The best thing I am doing now is simplifying things. I complicate things way too much, trying to be perfect. I'm just really enjoying playing now."

—Jonathan Byrd—2011 Hyundai Tournament of Champions

You Are In Control—Learn how to manage your own thoughts

TAKE CHARGE OF YOUR THOUGHTS

You may think that your emotional responses are reactions to somebody else's actions or external events, but I've got news for you—they're not! They are completely driven by your thoughts, bodily changes and behaviors.

We all have automatic conversations with ourselves. If you understand that negative, stressful thoughts have consequences, you know how important it is to control them. Any attitude or thought that diverts your attention away from

the now must be controlled or otherwise de-
flected. Any thoughts not directly focused on
getting the ball in the cup, letting the ball rip
with ease, and making the perfect shot are quite
simply irrational and in the way.

Commit yourself to identifying these useless
and irrational patterns of thinking, then, you can
stop them before they have a chance to trip you
up. Don't gossip. Don't retell an old story. If you
find yourself starting to complain, stop. It may
be difficult at first—these are, after all, mostly
subconscious acts. But the more you practice
thinking thoughts that serve you, the easier it all
becomes.

Remember, you're the one in control. You have
the power to redirect your thoughts. You can't
always determine what thoughts pop into your
head, but you ultimately choose what thoughts
you will dwell upon.

Research shows that high achievers have what's
called "positive self-expectancy." This means that
what is expected tends to be realized. If you

expect to win, you'll win. If you doubt your success (this is negative self-expectancy) you virtually assure that failure will come into the picture. Your brain and nervous system respond only to the images and information you provide them. So, if you give your brain only positive images and information, you will have positive results.

Similarly, every thought or idea creates a physical reaction. If fearful thoughts pop into your head, your heartbeat will speed up. Worry and anxiety can create physical tension. Over time, people under stress begin to carry themselves differently—their posture slumps, their eyes are downcast, their voice is sullen. But you ultimately control how you respond to various stimuli. Choose to respond positively and your performance will follow suit. By changing the way you think, you change the way you feel. In the process, you end up changing the way you behave.

TIPS FOR AVOIDING DISTORTED THINKING ON AND OFF THE GOLF COURSE—DO'S AND DON'TS

1. Stop negative thinking before it stops you.

- ○ Don't over generalize—avoid saying "always" and "never," and instead use "sometimes."

- ○ Stay away from destructive labeling—for example, "He's a jerk."

- ○ Avoid mind reading or assuming what others are thinking—it doesn't work.

- ○ Don't have rules about how others should act (Plato's "ought motive").

- ○ Don't inflate the significance of an event (avoid catastrophizing).

2. Develop constructive inner dialogues that are deliberate and productive.

- ○ Acknowledge the emotions that you feel AS emotions—for example, "I'm really angry at the caddie."—instead of mistaking them for fact.

○ Restate the generalization so it applies to just this particular situation ("sometimes" and "often", not "always" and "never").

○ Turn the destructive labeling into a thought that looks again at the situation.

○ Acknowledging positive attributes makes it easier to find a solution—for example, "Maybe I'll ask him specifically what he observed to make that comment."

To put it simply—In golf, you are either playing Consciously Outside "The Zone" or Playing Unconsciously in "The Zone".

Relax, Focus, Commit and Execute—How to try less and perform better

Stress often stops us from thinking about our performance at critical moments. You've probably heard of athletes "freezing up". How will you perform when the critical moment comes?

If you practice this new way of thinking on the course, you'll find it more difficult to be derailed by the stresses of everyday life. You'll still get attacked by stressful thoughts, but you'll be able to banish them quickly and easily so you can focus.

You'll also be much more relaxed, and this will enhance your performance. Playing golf in a relaxed state means better strength, dexterity, alertness and overall fitness. Small setbacks won't discourage you like they used to. It will be just you and your shot, and you'll be so focused on making it that nothing else will be able to bother you.

Another way to retrain your body's involuntary functions is to practice autogenic exercises, also known as self-hypnosis. It's useful for learning automatic physiological responses in the body that will benefit you. These responses build strength and also increase your level of relaxation, and this translates to a better performance. They will also enhance your commitment to succeeding in the game. Basically, self-hypnosis helps your body operate like a well-tuned machine.

It helps you to break old habits when you address the ball and initiate your swing. These can be hard to change voluntarily. As you learn new techniques and unlearn the old, you master the mind body connection and create new behaviors into your game like a better swing, a more confident stance, etc. You've added ease, calmness, finesse and relaxation to your golfing skills by giving your brain's neuropathways a new and improved script to work with.

How many of you have known people who have lost weight by some drastic diet or exercise means only to gain it all back plus even more? In most cases, that's because they haven't changed their subconscious set point. Our brain is comprised of neuropathways that have been created by repeated patterns of thoughts, beliefs, actions, and habits. That's why we can walk without thinking left, right, left, right. That's why we can jump on a bicycle after not riding for twenty years and pick it up. It's because we are tapping into the neuropathways of our past experience of riding a bike.

If you don't like the results you are witnessing with your weight, body, and health, then you must break the old patterns and old conditioning that's causing them. That means creating new neuropathways.

NASA has proven that breaking subconscious patterns takes 30 to 60 days of brain training. You see, if you do not "retrain" your subconscious brain at the same time you make the decision to lose weight you will, within very short order, return to your old weight patterns. In essence, this automatic "trigger" causes you to rationalize why you're not sticking with your diet or exercise plan, and basically forces you to revert to your old patterns and habits.

In order to install new more productive tapes or new neuropathways you must do things differently for 30/60/90 days.

If you can do this new behavior for 90 days, it will in most cases became a permanent lifestyle change. Remember, if you go through that same path every day for 30 days, there is a new pathway. The more you do it, the more ingrained the pathway is and thus the easier it will be to take this path over and over again. (1)

Practicing self-hypnosis and tapping in to the subconscious will take your performance to a whole new level. You have it in you already to teach your body to learn how to instantly relax. Each time you give yourself the cue, you experience a wave of relaxation that in turn triggers highly acute awareness, focus, clarity of mind and a deep sense of security in your body.

The best part about all of it is that it's no work at all. It's just a new way to communicate with yourself, a new way to master the mental game of golf. What makes hypnosis work so beautifully is that when we relax, our brainwaves shift to the Delta level. What this means is that we achieve a level of consciousness that we use in super learning.

Up until the age of two, we all experience this type of learning—we take things in instantly without reacting in any way. From ages two to twelve, we do most of our learning through Theta waves, which put us into a trance-like state. From age 12 onward, Beta waves dominate by helping us consciously maintain focus in class and at work.

What this means is simple—if you expose your-self to new information while undergoing hyp-nosis—experiencing it on the levels of Delta and Theta brainwaves—chances are high that you'll be able to create new responses. You are, in ef-fect, soaking up new information the way little kids do.

"When I play my best golf, I feel as if I'm in a fog, standing back watching the earth in orbit with a golf club in my hands."

—*Mickey Wright*

 ## Trust Yourself—Trust your mind, keep it simple and stay positive

There's no one else out there on the course but you, so you have to trust yourself innately and completely. The trust you have in your abilities, the ease of your movements, and the flow of your actions ultimately ensure your success when you swing your club. If you block that fundamental self-trust, your game and life both will suffer.

This personal sense of energy is critical in everything you do. Don't waste time measuring it or determining how effective it is, keep it as your own. Be aware of it and pay attention to the things that motivate you. You don't have to be perfectly relaxed to be optimally effective. Trust that you're relaxed enough to get out there and win.

Of course, you'll still sweat a bit. Your heart might race too. That's perfectly normal and some golfers even recognize it as a tangible sign of good stress, the stress that makes you perform. But use your knowledge of the relationship between your conscious and subconscious to control your performance. Don't overtly think about your swing. Trust in yourself that you've trained your subconscious to do the right thing when the moment comes.

Where attention goes, energy flows. So, instead of focusing on your swing, focus on your target. If you can do this, you'll remove the distractions that overthinking a swing can bring. Staying focused on the target lets your body perform the swing automatically. This, in turn, can lower your golf score.

Cue yourself to slow your heart rate, relax your breathing, and take the edge off your stress by returning to your naturally calm state. Over time, you'll get better at switching into and out of your relaxed state. Focus on the now and resist any thoughts that try to pull you away. Focus instead on what you want—and what you can do right now to achieve it. By trusting in yourself and recognizing that you and only you are in charge of your performance, you drive better and score lower.

You need to always TRUST and COMMIT to your visualization and goals 100% and set up to the ball immediately. When you visualize, your mind tells your body exactly what it needs to do—how to align itself and how much exertion is required to hit the ball whether it's down the fairway or putting on the green. If you have any doubt or uncertainty, those negative thoughts will manifest themselves into tension and affect the quality of your shot. Trust and commit fully, and then let go and allow your body and mind to make the shot you visualized.

AND, don't spend too much time over the ball. Set up to the ball *immediately*. If you spend more than 11 seconds over the ball, you are changing your physiological being and your mind's focus will be gone!

"I close my eyes and see the shot. I look at the ball and see the type of shot I have in my mind. I see it fly and then I see it land. It's a way of seeing the result before you do it. I visualize the end result."

-Annika Sorenstam

Focus—How to focus on success instead of failure

Do you think negative thoughts? Do you let fear dominate your day? It's easy to say, "Stop it." Unfortunately, it isn't as easy to actually stop.

Try creating a game plan for everything you do. Get a pen right now and think through what your goals are going to be. Writing them down helps you draw more consciousness to them. Be as detailed as you wish.

As you're writing, ask yourself what a perfect shot looks like. Start with a mental picture, because we think best visually. Explain what that picture looks like. Describe every detail you can think of. Describe the ball's trajectory, the precise line it follows, where and how it lands, and where it stops. Include any other aspect of the process that comes to mind. Through visualization, you give yourself a better target for relearning the requisite tasks when you go into your relaxed state.

This higher state of focus is the core foundation of your success. Continued self-encouragement drives improved self-awareness. Eventually, you believe in what you're describing and what you're repeatedly affirming to yourself because your conscious mind uses what's stored in your subconscious to accomplish the task at hand. You've effectively reprogrammed your subconscious with a higher quality script.

Just as important, you're much more resistant to losing focus when negative thoughts make their inevitable, if brief, appearance. You will have created strength of character that directly affects the quality and consistency of your golf game.

"The only answer to fear is preparation. The better prepared you are, the more confident you become."

-Jack Nicklaus

Your Inner Confidence—How to access your inner confidence whenever you need it

In the perfect golf swing, we've got forward motion, momentum and grace. But let's set that aside for a moment and think about something else.

Right now, think about something you're really good at, other than golf. Maybe you're a good cook, you're good with kids, or you play a musical instrument. It doesn't really matter what it is, just pick one and go. What does it look like when it's done well? What does it feel like to be doing this with such exceptional talent? Do you feel confident?

Remember that your subconscious mind is at least a million times more powerful than your conscious mind. Your conscious mind sends information to the subconscious, while the subconscious is the service mechanism—it simply carries out what you desire.

If you decide to walk across the room, your powerful subconscious puts the countless pieces together in the most expedient, elegant fashion. When you're cooking, your subconscious is leveraging everything you know about culinary arts. You can cook with ease and confidence.

The same thing applies in golf.

Imagine what a champion golfer might look like—or feel—while playing the round of his life. How does he move across the course? How does he carry himself? What does his breathing look like? How would you describe the confident look on his face?

Now, forget about the champion golfer. Look at yourself instead. Think about your best day on the course—and if you haven't had one lately, imagine it. How do you feel? How do you carry yourself? How relaxed are you?

Put yourself in the shoes of the champion we just spoke about and model your behaviors accordingly. Picture yourself shooting like a pro, and then confidently heading down the course to line up your next shot. Then imagine the contentment you feel as you calmly approach the green and think your way through the process.

As you combine the image and the contentment, you are commanding your subconscious mind to make it so—and in doing so turning your thoughts into reality.

The state of your game is irrelevant. It doesn't matter that you're not Tiger Woods. Whether or not you sink the shot is irrelevant. The point is that you feel the full, uplifting force of unbridled self-confidence.

And it's a benefit that extends well beyond the golf green. Anytime during the day, close your eyes and picture yourself taking that shot. Do it while you're walking the dog, preparing dinner, or waiting at a red light. That fundamentally good feeling is only an imaginative moment away.

This kind of thinking isn't as farfetched as it seems. If you do it often and deeply enough, you will eventually *be* it as well. Put yourself in the winner's circle, and not only will your performance eventually follow suit, but you will also have more fun and feel more fulfilled no matter what number you write on your score card.

"It does not matter how hard you work at your sport unless you work effectively and work on the right areas. All the hard work you do to race toward your athletic goals can backfire when you hit a brick wall of worry caused by fear of failure."

-Patrick Cohn, Ph.D.

7 Meaning—Nothing has any meaning except the meaning you give it

"If you have a hint of perfectionism, fear of failure, or lack of trust in your performance, you block your ability to find the zone of effortless performance".

-Patrick Cohn, Ph.D.

The only thing that stands between you and mastery—of golf, of life, of anything at all—is fear. Instead of fearing your obstacles, open yourself to them and embrace them. In that way you'll pass right through them and be able to move on unencumbered. The obstacles in your path are only obstacles because you haven't mastered them yet. Indeed, they aren't obstacles at all—you simply *see* them as obstacles. Your fear has become your resistance. All resistance, then, is fear.

In order to stop fear of failure, the first thing you have to do is identify what type of fear makes you bang your head against the imaginary wall of worry. Most of these fears come from your intense desire to succeed, and your desire to avoid negative social scrutiny.

Most golfers and athletes with fear of failure are afraid to fail because they work so hard to achieve their goals. This intense desire to succeed causes both athletes and especially golfers, to worry about not getting what they badly want.

Many golfers and athletes become so worried about not achieving (or gaining social recognition) that they think too much about avoiding failure.

The next step in breaking through the wall of worry is to focus your mind on striving for success instead of avoiding failure. When you focus your mind on obtaining success, you will come much closer to getting what you want.

Finally, make sure that all the mental pictures or movies in your mind help you strive for success rather than avoid failure.

By leveraging the techniques of self-hypnosis or meditation, you give yourself the ability to turn doubt, fear, and worry into dim, distant memories. Beliefs that might have held you back can no longer do so. Released from your fear, you're more open to experiencing the things you've always wanted to experience—but were too afraid to try.

We ultimately live out of what we believe. So if you believe you can, you're right. Likewise, if you believe you can't, you're also right. What we believe can either give us a lot of energy, or it can give us none. The choice is yours.

So take the time to ask yourself some hard questions. "Who am I? What is true about me?" As you learn more about yourself—and the erroneous wholehearted beliefs you possess—you'll be in a better position to zero in on your beliefs, and to identify the thought patterns that stop you dead in your tracks.

Life, after all, is very much like a game. The challenges we face are like puzzle pieces. As we master each one, it's up to us to move on to the next and figure it out as well. Each piece of the puzzle creates a new wonder—a new now. And putting those puzzle pieces together isn't as impossible as it seems. All it takes is a few well targeted behavioral traits to help you develop an unquestionable belief that you will succeed:

- ○ Believe you are a winner and give all things that meaning.

- ○ Know that any effort you make—however small—will be greatly rewarded.

- ○ Strive for optimism, enthusiasm, self discipline, positive excitement, and adventure.

- ○ Strengthen and tune the mind to react to stimulus as you choose.

It doesn't take all that long for you to cultivate these mental skills. As a result, you'll get a sense of relaxation—in mind and in body—that will sharpen your mind. You'll be better able to focus on the ball, the target and your intended trajectory.

And, once you've applied this training to your golf game, it's just a small extra jump to do the same in your everyday life. Personal growth is based on learning something new every day, on finding wonder in every aspect of life. This heightened sense of focus, awareness, and relaxation represents a winning combination for golf. Just remember that its benefits also go well beyond the golf course.

> "People are always telling me I should do one thing or another, I should change my grip or shorten my swing. I should practice more and goof around less. I shouldn't smile on Sunday … I should … I shouldn't … Frankly I don't know why they worry. It's my life—and I don't worry."
>
> *-Fred Couples*

Breathing—How to breathe through your eyes

"Breathing through your eyes" isn't as confusing as it sounds. What it means is that personal growth is all about opening yourself to new experiences. We open our eyes in different ways, and figuratively breathe through them. Doing this, we absorb information differently and increase our personal potential. In everything we do, we're surrounded by energy. It's up to us to use every sense we have to somehow capture it.

You likely already do this and may not even be aware of it. Do you zone in and out? Do you ever find yourself in an alternative state of consciousness? Breathing through your eyes means purposefully moving into and out of this state—doing it with increased awareness.

This matters because we all have moments where everything comes together with absolute perfection. For example, a round where every shot felt solid and you could do no wrong with your clubs. Unfortunately, when we think back on the experience after the fact, we try to recreate that magic and it always fails. We try to schedule another round with the same foursome, the same golf cart, even the same set of socks. And it doesn't pan out. What went wrong?

Our approach is what's wrong. We mistakenly assume the magic is in the locations, the conditions, the players. In fact, the magic is within us and how we were thinking at the time. Fortunately, now we can master the way we think and control the relationship between the conscious and subconscious mind. As a result, we're better able to put our minds in the right place, the same place we were when we shot that memorable round.

Once you hit the course with this new, more re-laxed and open mindset, anything becomes pos-sible. Your newfound trust in your potential allows you to breathe through your eyes and believe, to the depth of your soul, that anything is possible today.

This paradigm shift isn't limited to your eyes, ei-ther. Imagine experiencing the world uniquely through another sense and similar possibilities become apparent. You feel only because of what you're thinking—not because of circumstance or those who surround you. While this can unde-niably help your game, more importantly it in-creases your enjoyment of the experience. You bring newfound energy to the experience, which can benefit you and those around you in so many other ways.

In the end, it doesn't matter that the eye isn't capable of actually breathing. If you imagine that it's even possible, then you've opened your mind to new possibilities on and off the course. So close your eyes, and imagine what it would be like if you could even take a tiny breath through them. The result, as you may imagine, is eye-opening!

As an exercise and especially while playing a round and the pressure is on, breathing deeply helps you relax and focus. Normally, we breathe deeply through our noses but now you can take it up a notch by visualizing using your eyes instead of your nose. A deeper state of relaxation will occur and your focus becomes clearer.

"Change your thoughts and change your world"

- Norman Vincent Peale

Your Success Scorecard— Keeping track of your successes

You'll never know how well you're doing unless you track it daily and celebrate the results. Acknowledge that you are already doing many things right. Otherwise, you would not have reached your present level of success. Reward yourself for your successes.

Learn from your mistakes and be prepared to change your approach if it's not working for you. This may involve changing or strengthening your patterns of physiology, behavior, and cognition.

When you change or strengthen your habits, you encourage the brain to learn to control itself. These don't have to be huge changes. Take the time to give yourself a simple pat on the back even if all you did was take a baby step. Any step forward, however small, is still a step forward, so don't miss an opportunity to recognize it.

When you're away from the golf course, commit yourself to spending two to three minutes at various points throughout the day visualizing your on-course activities. Run through your successful golf scenarios again and again until they're set into your subconscious. Focus only on succeeding and quickly get rid of any thoughts of failure. If you think of failure, your performance will immediately suffer.

While it is important to actually get out there and practice the game itself, thinking it through when you have a free moment is just as important a factor in reaching a higher level of performance. Learn to integrate both on and off course activities and thinking, because in the end, they're all inextricably related. Focus on perfect

putts and perfect chips; live in kindness, grateful-
ness, and success; live in your mind the life you
seek and eliminate negativity. Following this ho-
listic life philosophy will determine the amount
of success and abundance you will have.

Before you go to sleep at night, make an effort
write down the things you are grateful for and
the behaviors you know are helping you grow
as a person and as a golfer. Review your affirmations for success now, and again first thing in the
morning. And when you do reach a milestone
along your journey, don't hesitate to reward
yourself. An ice cream tastes that much sweeter
when it's been well earned.

> They say, "practice" makes perfect." Of course,
> it doesn't. For the vast majority of golfers it
> merely consolidates imperfection.
>
> *- Henry Longhurst*

The Problem With Perfection— What's wrong with perfection and why you should never give up

Your mother was right—practice does indeed make perfect. If you're going to effectively reap the benefits of this book, you have to visualize the end result, formulate the plan for achieving the result and simplifying "things". It's how professionals in any sport become professionals in the first place. They weren't born at the top of their game. They spent years practicing, sacrificing and, yes, failing before they had the right to call themselves pros. It takes commitment over time if you want to raise your win percentage and your enjoyment factor.

If you take persistent and consistent action, winning will follow. Be persistent and consistent with your thoughts, beliefs, affirmations, positive nature, plans and goals.

I know that you can do it. Don't ever give up on yourself, on your game or on anything. If this were something difficult, I'd understand why some people couldn't do it. But it's not difficult at all, it just takes some commitment. If you're committed, there is no work at all. This method is all about making life easier, not harder.

These ten golden rules are designed to escort your mind to where you want it to go. They get you there by having fun and creating new thought and action habits to help you attain your goals. And don't forget to cut out the page at the back of this book, laminate it and keep it with you in your golf bag, referring to it often during your round.

The only things I want you to give up are the self-limiting beliefs that, over the years, have become your mantra of "I can't." Give up the idea that your mind is always right.

Give up self-doubt. Give up any resistance to the idea that you are capable of expanding, enriching, enjoying, and excelling. Give up the notion that you are a victim. Instead, have what you want now. Be it now.

Never give up on your fabulous imagination. Use it constructively and often. Truly begin to imagine what it is like to step into the perfect image of you. Think about your best day, and then make it happen in your mind. Before you know it, it will no longer be a reality only in your mind. It will be a reality, period.

You can't be perfect with your mental focus. No one is perfect. Not even Tiger Woods. But he is the master at refocusing and regaining his concentration after he slips.

The mental strategy of refocusing should not take you longer than 2-4 seconds to complete in competition. The sooner you can refocus—the better your concentration and performance will be!

Points to Ponder and Remember

"May you live all the days of your life"

-*Jonathan Swift*

Using the new mental techniques presented to you in this book, you are now equipped to avoid upsets by using communication and understanding effectively. These approaches will provide you with the tools to build self confidence, consistency and control.

Make the positive decision to be a winner. Play by the rules. Trust and respect yourself. As you walk down the fairway, look around to take in the lovely scenery, because the only time you need to focus is at the moment you play your shot.

Take in the precious moments of beauty in your life. That's the right way to professionalism, the right way to golf and most importantly, the right way to life.

> "Think like a man of action, act like a man of thought"
>
> —*Henri Bergson*

You are a life force. You generate life by making decisions. You generate action by carrying out your decisions. Only by setting a goal or aiming at a target can you achieve your goals.

Excellence is a process. You have to believe this and understand this in order to get through the lulls of your own game. When you understand that adversity is built into golf, you don't get frustrated when it visits you. You simply work through your adversity with patience, a supremely positive attitude and confidence. (Gary Player, a Hall of Famer has invented an entire language of euphemisms to avoid saying any-thing remotely negative).

There is no "avoiding" the lulls in the game; there is only learning from them. I totally believe and espouse that "Competency is the ability to dance during breakdown (c)".

First of all, golf is not about perfection. You can hit poor shots but still have great results. The sec-ond, and CRITICALLY important lesson, is to work as much on your short game and wedges as you do on your full swing. That simple fact plays out year after year in golf on every level. A great short game makes you a match for any oppo-nent. If you ignore your short game and wedges, it really doesn't matter how "good" your mechan-ical swing is (the Tour is full of technically perfect golf swings ... but what gets golfers to the win-ner's circle is what they do from inside 110 yards).

They're called "scoring clubs" for a reason.

Having a singular focus on a routine is really im-portant. You need a solid routine that has been designed to counteract the variability that takes

place around a golfer. More important, the routine is NOT about doing the same things in the
same order. More accurately, it is about DOING
THE SAME THINGS IN THE SAME ORDER WITH THE SAME
RHYTHM AND TENSION. The focus for competitive
golfers should typically be 90% process and 10%
results and positioning.

Wherever you place your attention, that is where
you give life and power. So, if you focused your
attention on avoiding hitting out of bounds,
missing a putt or shunning a bunker, instead
of concentrating on sinking the putt etc. that is
where your energy will be directed.

The one thing holding you back from achieving
your potential is a negative thought, brought
on by one or any combination of the following:
fear, anxiety, nervousness, doubt, uncertainty
and most importantly, mistrust in your ability to
bring things about simply by making decisions.

When you give into these emotions and compromise yourself, you go against the attitude
you know you should be concentrating on—a

positive one! It is this compromise that causes all the failures, disappointments and goofed shots. Understanding that a slight negative thought can impact on your game, how it affects your aim, natural rhythm, flow and score, is the first step towards controlling the outcome of future play. Once you are aware, you gain control of your targets and goals.

Merely by making a positive decision and having complete trust in that decision, you can make it happen.

Trust your positive decisions. Decisions do not contain any force or effort. It is unnecessary to try and force your shots. This will cause you to go off line. Likewise, do not deliberately try to slow your swing. You already have your own natural speed. In fact, every golfer has their own speed of playing, whether it is fast, medium or slow. Once you are aware of your target, your movements will be entirely natural.

Place your attention on how to execute the shot and you will get the result of where you placed your attention. In other words, by focusing on the target and having the attention to attain your target, you will lower your score and achieve your goals more often.

Never compromise yourself when playing golf. Take no risk or chance while playing, especially if you know that it has no real possibility of being to your advantage. If you take a risk, beware of the consequences and take responsibility for the outcome.

Once you decide on your target, don't think about how you are going to execute the shot. Just make the decision to hit the target. Remember, if your attention is focused on making a good putt, well, then, you'll make a good putt. But wouldn't you rather hole the putt? If you are in doubt about your putting stroke or the line of the putt, your attention is not on the target, and your intention is not really on holing the putt. Obviously your chances of success are less.

Golf is a game of intention, commitment, attention and responsibility. Live in the present time and be aware. This means actively noticing and observing your immediate environment. Forget about past mistakes and future uncertainties. Don't worry about goofed shots or shots that still have to be played. Be willing to accept the result of whatever action you have chosen, good or bad, and play each shot as you come to it— totally relaxed, totally focused, at ease and with confidence.

Golf is also a game of estimation and judgment. When selecting the correct club, your first selection is the correct one. Do not doubt your decision because you will introduce negative thought into your shot. This also applies to the first reading of a putt. While you are reading the putt, visualize the exact spot where the putt will dive into the hole. Use positive mental images to guide you to what you know can happen.

No matter what others may advise you, trust in your own reality. You always know what is good for you. The penalty of compromising yourself is failure, disappointment, frustration, confusion and lack of confidence.

Set a low target for each round. Set a low score because you know low scores are possible. Take courage, be positive—don't worry about how you are going to achieve that low score. Just play each shot as you come to it. Be aware only of the present. "Breathe through your eyes", deeply to relax before each shot. By doing this, low scores will just happen.

Do what you can with the total confidence of a person who deserves success! In golf and in life, use positive mental images to guide you to what you know can happen.

Remember, a clear head is essential for a stress free body. You can achieve clarity by communicating honestly and actively at all times, by taking total responsibility for everything and never compromising yourself or your integrity. The right way to golf is the right way to life, so do what you know you can do with confidence and trust.

When you are totally committed to these vital points, you will naturally achieve scores lower than you have ever achieved before AND you will have the right mind for golf!

The Right Mind for Golf
Mastering Your Mental Game
Barry Lotz, Ph.D., J.D.

This card should be kept in your golf bag or yardage book. Consulting these Positive thoughts throughout your round will reap benefits but more importantly, allow you to shoot your lowest scores, and, at the very least, place you in the Top Ten in every tournament! You can obtain an original laminated card by emailing Dr. Lotz at drlotz@cbsgolf.net.

○ **Relax, Concentrate & Execute**

- ○ Prepare to play—practice relaxation before and during a round. BREATHE rhythmically.

- ○ Focus on the process and take your mind off the result.

- ○ Concentrate by settling down into yourself— pure focus by getting lost in the game.

- ○ Develop your mental and physical pre-shot routine.

- ○ Stay with manageable goals.

○ **Play One Shot at a Time**

- ○ Increase your concentration on the present moment.

- ○ Visualize the path of the ball to a SPECIFIC target both on long and short shots.

- ○ See and feel both the swing and the path of the shot.

- ○ Be CLEAR and COMMITTED to each shot. Back away if at all uncomfortable!

- A round of golf is a series of separate and unique performances.

- Allow your great swings and performances to emerge!

- Believe in yourself.

❍ Manage Your Emotions

- Accept your play on every shot.

- Isolate each hole regardless of how you felt when you walked off the previous green.

- Stay with your routine.

- Learn how to stay on an even keel.

❍ Believe in Yourself

- Trust your instincts, your thoughts and your swing.

- Allow yourself to WIN.

❍ Smart Course Management Skills are Imperative.

- Have the courage and fortitude to make prudent decisions.

- Be patient—believe that things will come around your way.

- Stay Positive and Have Fun.

Dr. Lotz is one of the leading speakers, writers and researchers on mental strategies for winning golf. He works with numerous Tour Pros and committed golfers of all abilities. He holds a PGA Instructor badge and is president of the Professional Golf Teachers Association of America. He can be reached in La Quinta, CA at 760.777.1925 or drlotz@cbsgolf.net

APPENDIX

GMAP—PART 1

Golfer's Mental Aptitude Profile (GMAP)
Part 1

Name:	Email:	Phone:

Directions: *Please answer the following questions about your mental approach to golf. Please be honest and specific with your answers. Your answers will help me to improve your mental game of golf. Also, provide a brief description of your golf background and any statistics you have kept in the last year.*

1. What are your long-term goals for golf (1-2 years)? Be specific. What interim practice or performance goals do you need to achieve in order to reach your long-range goals?	
2. What are your biggest mental challenges in golf that hold you back in which you are aware of? What are your specific objectives for mental game coaching? Please explain.	

3. Rate your level of motivation to achieve your goals (from 1-10)? If you think that you lack motivation, what beliefs, ideas, or other people sabotage your motivation?	
4. What events, limiting beliefs, or expectations you maintain, hold you back from reaching your goals?	
5. What motivates you to succeed in golf: (1) love of the game, fun of competition, or to achieve personal goals, or (2) to get trophies, acknowledgement, or to gain the respect of people in my life?	
6. Describe your attitude and behavior when you are in "the zone" or playing your best?	
7. Describe your attitude and behavior when not playing well? Compare this to when you play your best. What are the biggest differences?	

8. How would you rate your level of confidence today that you can play well (from 1-10)? If you do not rate yourself as a "10," what doubts or beliefs hold you back from having high confidence?	
9. Rate your level of confidence (from 1-10) in the various parts of your game (driver, iron play, putting, chipping, pitching, sand play, etc)? Select 1 to 10 on the boxes to the right.	Driver Iron play Putting Chipping Pitching Sand play Course Management Other
10. How <u>sturdy</u> or <u>fragile</u> is your confidence? Do you lose confidence easily after a poor shot, hole, or round? What events or situations cause you to lose your self-confidence in golf?	

11. How often do you have "doubt" before, during, and after each round (0%--100% of the time)? In what situations do you doubt the most? What thoughts do you have when you doubt yourself?	
12. (a) How often do you have lapses in concentration during play? (b) What are your major sources of distractions in golf, both internal distractions (*such as negative thinking*) and external (*such as others talking during your shot*)?	
13. When not playing up to your ability, do you stay composed and "grind out" the round to shoot the best score possible, or do you lose emotional control or lose interest during the round?	

14. Do you think you perform better in practice (on the range) than in competition (on the course)? If so, how does your attitude/behavior change when you go from a practice situation to competition?	
15. Do other activities in your life (school, job, spouse, relationships, etc.) distract your from playing your best and not allow you to focus solely on golf? What activities in your life are distractions to golfing?	
16. What expectations do you have before you play a competitive round? Do you expect to hit the ball perfect, putt well, or achieve a target score? List your common expectations.	

17. When playing better than expected, do you have problems finishing off a round (does your "comfort zone" prevent you from going low or breaking scoring barriers)?	
18. Does fear of failure, anxiety, or tension prevent you from playing your best? What are your biggest fears or pressures that affect your performance? Please explain.	
19. Are you able to make a relaxed and free swing in competition? Or do you guide, steer, or over-control your swing or stroke when competing? When do you guide, steer, or over-control the swing?	

20. How dedicated are you to training and improving your game by working closely with your coach, improving your mental game, improving fitness and health, and practicing effectively? What is missing in your training program?	
21. What else do you want to say about your mental game of golf? (Use the other side if necessary)	

APPENDIX
GMAP—PART 2

Golfer's Mental Aptitude Profile (GMAP) Part 2

Directions: Please answer each question with a number (1-7) next to each statement that best describes your situation.

(1) Never (2) Very Rarely (3) Rarely (4) Sometimes (5) Often (6) Very Often (7) Always

CONFIDENCE

1. I am confident in my ability to perform more than other golfers I compete with.

2. I can quickly regain my confidence after a couple of poor rounds.

3. Other people have confidence in me because they know I'm the best.

4. I embrace the pressure to make a putt on the last hole to win a match.

5. My confidence remains high even after a bad shot or big number on a hole.

COMPOSURE UNDER PRESSURE

1. My confidence thrives when the tournament or match is mine to win or lose.

2. I can easily forget mistakes and play on without dwelling on them.

3. I stay composed when I make an error or stupid mistake.

4. In pressure situations, I am able to play free without fear.

5. I perform better when the pressure to produce is on.

CONCENTRATION

1. When others talk to me, I get distracted by my own thoughts.

2. I get pulled off task when outside distractions are present.

3. It's hard for me to stay focused for 30 seconds during my preshot preparation.

4. I think about my score and end results; I have trouble focusing on the process.

5. I focus worse when I have to make a critical shot or putt in competition.

COMMITMENT

1. I am more dedicated and committed to golf than most golfers I know.

2. I like the feelings that come with playing in a close competition.

3. Working hard in practice to get better is gratifying.

4. I feel the best when playing golf compared to any other activity.

5. I sacrifice doing other activities because of my dedication to golf.

MOTIVATIONAL TENDENCIES

1. I work on mechanics and use more time to perfect my skills than other golfers use.

2. I want to win so badly that I get tense, anxious, and steer my swing.

3. I enjoy practicing golf more so than I enjoy playing.

4. I have high expectations for my performance.

5. I become frustrated when I don't perform up to my expectations.

Golfer's Mental Aptitude Profile (GMAP)
Part 2

(1) Never (2) Very Rarely (3) Rarely (4) Sometimes (5) Often (6) Very Often (7) Always

ROUTINES

1. I have a specific routine I follow for each shot, putt, and chip.

2. I am aware of the moment I get out of my normal routine.

3. I commit to the club and know what shot I will hit before addressing each shot.

4. My mental and physical routine feels natural and effortless to perform.

5. When I get distracted or have doubt, I stop and restart the routine over.

CONFIDENCE & PRACTICE

1. I am confident that I practice efficiently and work on the right things.

2. Practice gives me confidence and I can take that confidence to the course.

3. I derive confidence from my training program and effective practice.

4. I use practice to become a more confident player, not to just beat balls.

5. My confidence remains high even after a sloppy practice session.

PRACTICE ROUTINES

1. I have a set practice schedule or routine that I follow every week.

2. When I practice, I have a specific purpose and goals I accomplish.

3. When I practice, I can't get as intensely focused as I am in competition.

4. I practice my short game as much as if not more than I practice my long game.

5. I perform as well as or better in tournaments rounds as I do in practice rounds.

SOCIAL APPROVAL

1. One of my goals is to impress others with my golf skills.

2. Gaining the respect and admiration from fellow golfers is important to me.

3. I worry about embarrassing myself in front of other who are watching my game.

4. Getting acknowledged in the media (paper, TV) for my golf is very satisfying.

5. I wonder how others judge my game and think of me.

GAME IMPROVEMENT

1. I set a regular schedule to work with my golf coach on my technique.

2. I work with a sports psychologist or read mental game books to improve my game.

3. I improve my fitness by working out and stretching three times or more per week.

4. I eat well and watch my diet on and off the golf course.

5. I study the golf course and set a game plan before I play a tournament round.

6. I use a specific warm up routine to prepare for every competitive round I play.

*Please email your completed GMAP to
drlotz@cbsgolf.net or fax to 760.406.9898.*

*There is a $795.00 fee to send you a Mental
Analysis and Game Plan*

The Right Mind For Golf © Dr. Barry Lotz in
association with Peak Performance Sports © &
Dr. Patrick Cohn

Optimism + Gratitude - Less Ego = Success

The Knots Daily Affirmation

Untie the knots
that are in my mind,
my heart and my life.
Remove all the have nots,
The can nots and the do nots
That I have in my mind.

Erase the will nots,
may nots,
might nots that may find
a home in my heart.

Release me from the could nots,
would nots and
should nots that obstruct my life.

And most of all,
Allow me to remove from my mind,
my heart and my life all of the 'am nots'
that I have allowed to hold be back,
especially the thought
That I am not good enough.

Self hypnosis is really a skill you can develop through repetition, learning to achieve total relaxation, and the use of constant self-affirmations.

STEPS TO PERFORM SELF HYPNOSIS

1. First, decide what you wish to accomplish with this session of self hypnosis. For example, you may plan to give yourself autosuggestions that will increase your self-confidence and poise for an upcoming golf tournament or interview. Create one or two positive sentences toward this end, making sure to frame them in the present tense: *"I am gracious, charismatic and confident of my golf skills and talent"* might be one possibility.

2. Highly recommended is the writing out your suggestions before performing the hypnosis. This can be very effective, as a visual list of what you choose to work on can sometimes be more easily remembered than even carefully assembled thoughts.

3. Next, choose a quiet, private place to per-
    form your self hypnosis. A dark room or quiet
    area is recommended. Plan at least half an
    hour without interruption.

4. Sit in a comfortable chair. You may prefer a
    chair whose back is high enough so that you
    can lean back comfortably against it. Sitting
    is preferable to lying down, unless your goal
    is to fall asleep.

5. Close your eyes and breathe deeply at least
    three times. Use the "Breathe through your
    Eyes" technique mentioned in the book. Tell
    yourself to relax completely. One way to as-
    sist the process of full relaxation is to tighten
    your muscles, hold for about four seconds,
    and then relax them fully. Relax each part of
    your body, beginning with your face, your
    neck, your shoulders, etc.

6. Now imagine yourself in an elevator, going
    slowly down, floor by floor. Count silently as
    you reach each floor: Ten, Nine, Eight....

7. When you reach One, the door of the elevator will open, and you will find yourself in a room. Tell yourself that you will find whatever you need in that room. Begin your self suggestions at this point. You may simply picture yourself doing, or being, or experiencing, whatever is your goal for this session.

8. Continue to breathe deeply and evenly as you repeat these suggestions. You may even wish to say them out loud a couple of times.

9. When you feel ready, imagine yourself entering the elevator again, and its door closing behind you. This time count up, as the elevator moves slowly upward: One, Two, Three, etc.

10. When you reach Ten, you will open your eyes slowly. You control your mind during this process, and your constant self-affirmations have a powerful effect for change on your subconscious mind.

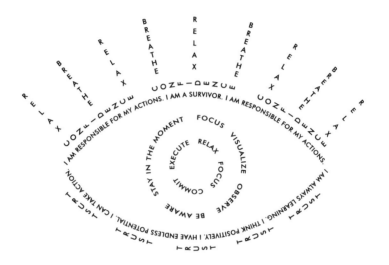

OPTIMISM + GRATITUDE - EGO = SUCCESS